Magic, Myth, and Mystery

WITCHES

DO YOU BELIEVE?

This series features creatures that excite our minds. They're magical. They're mythical. They're mysterious. They're also not real. They live in our stories. They're brought to life by our imaginations. Facts about these creatures are based on folklore, legends, and beliefs. We have a rich history of believing in the impossible. But these creatures only live in fantasies and dreams. Monsters do not live under our beds. They live in our heads!

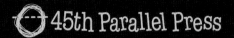
45th Parallel Press

Published in the United States of America by Cherry Lake Publishing
Ann Arbor, Michigan
www.cherrylakepublishing.com

Reading Adviser: Marla Conn MS, Ed., Literacy specialist, Read-Ability, Inc.
Book Design: Felicia Macheske

Photo Credits: © Onigiri studio/Shutterstock.com, cover; © Alexander Erdbeer/Shutterstock.com, 1;
© Dieter Spears/iStock, 5; © Nomad_Soul/Shutterstock.com, 7; © Khomenko Maryna/Shutterstock.com, 8;
© Estremo/Shutterstock.com, 11; © Captblack76/Shutterstock.com, 12; © iordani/Shutterstock.com, 15;
© Lario Tus/Shutterstock.com, 17; © Kotin/Shutterstock.com, 18; © KI Petro/Shutterstock.com, 20; © KI
Petro/Shutterstock.com, 20; © CREATISTA/Shutterstock.com, 23; © Gergely Zsolnai/Shutterstock.com, 24;
© Khomenko Maryna/Shutterstock.com, 27; © Dundanim/Shutterstock.com, 29

Graphic Elements Throughout: © denniro/Shutterstock.com; © Libellule/Shutterstock.com; © sociologas/
Shutterstock.com; © paprika/Shutterstock.com; © ilolab/Shutterstock.com; © Bruce Rolff/Shutterstock.com

45th Parallel Press is an imprint of Cherry Lake Publishing.

Library of Congress Cataloging-in-Publication Data

Names: Loh-Hagan, Virginia, author.
Title: Witches : magic, myth, and mystery / by Virginia Loh-Hagan.
Description: Ann Arbor : Cherry Lake Publishing, [2016] | Series: Magic,
 myth, and mystery | Includes bibliographical references and index.
Identifiers: LCCN 2016004928| ISBN 9781634711128 (hardcover) | ISBN
 9781634713108 (pbk.) | ISBN 9781634712118 (pdf) | ISBN 9781634714099
 (ebook)
Subjects: LCSH: Witches—Juvenile literature. | Witchcraft—Juvenile
 literature.
Classification: LCC BF1566 .L64 2016 | DDC 398.21—dc23
LC record available at http://lccn.loc.gov/2016004928

Cherry Lake Publishing would like to acknowledge the work of The Partnership for 21st Century Skills.
Please visit *www.p21.org* for more information.

Printed in the United States of America
Corporate Graphics Inc.

TABLE of CONTENTS

Chapter One

Wicked or Good?

What are witches? What are some types of witches? What do witches look like?

"I'll get you, my pretty. And your little dog, too!" The Wicked Witch of the West said this. She's from *The Wizard of Oz*. She's wicked. But there are good witches, too.

Witches are special humans. They practice magic. They have powers. They have skills. They can be men or women. **Warlocks** are male witches. They're usually evil.

Covens are groups of witches. Most covens have 13 witches. Witches meet. They get together. They do witchcraft. Some witches work alone. They're called hedge witches.

Wizards are wise. Some say they're more powerful than witches.

Explained by Science!

Many witches are believed to fly on broomsticks. This can be explained. Brooms are symbols of the home. Women used to do the cleaning. They were connected to brooms. Some women were accused of being witches. They made "flying potions" or "witches' brew." They used herbs and plants. Some plants have poison. Examples are deadly nightshade and mandrake. The potion looked like green goop. These accused witches rubbed the potion on broomsticks. They rubbed the potion into their bodies. (Absorbing the potion through skin increases the effects.) They ate the potion. They had other people eat the potion. The potion caused hallucinations. Hallucinations are like wild dreams. People saw things that weren't there. They felt like they were flying. They felt like they were floating.

There are many kinds of witches. White witches do good magic. They help people. Black witches do bad magic. They harm people. Gray witches are good and bad.

Witch doctors heal. They use things from nature. They fight against evil **spirits**.

Sea witches command the sea. They control the moon. They control tides. They control weather. They steer ships. They decide whether sailors will live or die.

Kitchen witches protect homes.

Traditional witches work with spirits. Spirits are from another world.

Some witches are pretty. Some are ugly. Some change. Some look like people. Some look like monsters. Witches come in all shapes. They come in all sizes.

Some witches are green. They wear black robes. They wear pointy hats. They have hooked noses. They have warts. They have knobby fingers. They're **hags**. Hags are old women.

Some witches have moles. They have birthmarks. They have scars. They have extra body parts.

Some witches fly. They fly on brooms. They ride flying animals.

Some witches talk to themselves.

Chapter Two

Casting Spells and More!

What powers do witches have?
What tools do witches use?

Witches **cast spells**. They create magical actions. There are different spells. Spells banish. They repel. They protect. They harm.

There are different ways to cast spells. Witches say special words. They do special things. They use **runes**. These are stones with symbols. They use **wands**. Wands are magical sticks.

Witches can store spells. First, they start a spell. They save the last words. They wait for the right time.

Then, they finish the spell with the magic words.
Witches **hex**. Hex means to give curses. They
wish for bad things. They also give **blessings**.
Blessings are good wishes.

Some witches make a "sacred circle." This is where they do magic.

Witches make **potions**. Potions are special mixes. Some potions poison people. Some potions make people do things. Love potions are popular.

Witches use **cauldrons**. These are big cooking pots. They're black. They have three legs. They cook potions.

Witches use **charms**. These are magical objects. They have power. They do specific tasks.

Some witches have **psychic** powers. Psychic means the mind. These witches see the past. They see the future. They read minds. They **scry**. Scrying is gazing. Witches gaze into crystal balls. They gaze into mirrors. They gaze into candles. They gaze into water. They wait for **visions**. Visions are signs. They're messages.

The witching hour is when witches are most powerful. It's around 3:15 a.m.

When Fantasy Meets Reality!

Aye-ayes live in Madagascar. They're active at night. They look odd. They're a collection of body parts. They have rat heads. They have beaver teeth. They have bat ears. They have fox tails. They have monkey bodies. And they have witches' hands. Their fingers are skinny. They're knotty. Aye-ayes have long, bony middle fingers that are three times longer than other fingers. Some people believe ayes-ayes do evil witch work. They think ayes-ayes predict death. They're scared when ayes-ayes point their middle fingers. They think this means the person will die. Some people believe aye-ayes creep into houses. Then, they dig their fingers into people's chests. Next, they pierce people's hearts. People killed them. They ate them. They wanted to take away the bad luck. But aye-ayes are harmless. They're gentle. And they're not witches.

Some witches have animals. These animals are **familiars**. They're more than pets. They serve their witches. They do things witches can't. They go places witches can't.

The most popular are black cats. These cats have nine lives. They're demons. They spy. Some witches can turn into their cats.

Witches love honeybees. They use their wax. They make figures. This is for black magic. Witches love wolves. They ride wolves. Witches love toads. Toads are used in potions. They're used as charms.

Some witches can speak to animals.

15

Chapter Three

Witchy Weaknesses

What are witches' weaknesses? What are some limitations to witches' powers? What is the Witch's Creed?

There are ways to stop witches' spells. It's harder to stop a witch. Witches are strong. But they have weaknesses.

Witches don't like knots. They don't like **braids**. Braids are things woven together. Braids trap witches' gazes. Witches don't like all herbs. Some herbs hurt witches. These include rosemary, fennel, and rue. Witches don't like salt. Salt burns their skin. They don't like iron. Iron weakens their magic.

Water melts some witches. Some witches can't cross water.

Some witches are stronger than others.

Magic has rules. Witches cast spells by talking. They say words out loud. So, gagging witches makes them powerless. Some spells require witches to see. Some require touch. So, blocking witches makes them powerless.

Some witches have **power caps**. There's a limit to their power. Witches are born with power. They only have a certain amount. This is all they'll have. They can't gain more power. They can't create more power.

Strong spells take a lot of energy. They take a lot of work. Witches get tired. They can drain their power. They can kill themselves.

SURVIVAL TIPS!

- Witches' curses cause bad dreams. Find pebbles. The pebbles must have holes. (They're called hagstones.) The holes deflect the bad dreams. String the stones together. Hang it in your bedroom window.

- Invoke the "Light of the Divine." Chant special words. Do this five times a day.

- Make a "witch's bottle." It also sends back evil. Find a jar. Fill it halfway with sharp objects. Add hair or nail clippings. Fill it to the top. Put the top on. Seal it with tape. Bury it in the ground at least 12 inches (30.5 centimeters) deep. You're safe if the bottle stays buried and unbroken.

- Make a witch cake. Feed it to a dog. This hurts witches. They'll cry out in pain.

Witches can't hide from each other. They know upon sight. They know upon touch.

Witches have a **creed**. A creed is a rule. It's the "Threefold Law." Witches can do evil deeds. But the evil comes back to them. It comes back three times more. The same goes for good deeds. Witches must think before they act.

Some witches command nature. They control the weather. But this is dangerous. It's hard magic. Weather is powerful. There can be bad results. Witches can't control what happens.

A popular saying for witches is "Ever mind the rule of three."

Chapter Four

Born or Learned

What are hereditary witches? How do witches learn or develop their skills?

There are two ways to become a witch. Witches are born witches. Or they learn to be witches.

Hereditary witches are born witches. They have witch blood. They inherit certain magical skills. They have witch parents. Or they have witch grandparents. They're taught by their families. They learn from a young age. They can create their own spells.

Some can become witches. They learn from a hereditary witch. They can't create their own spells. They cast spells made by others.

Each witch family has their own spells, beliefs, and practices.

All witches need training. Witchcraft is a developed skill. It takes time. It takes practice.

Witches start as **apprentices**. Apprentices are learners. They learn from **mentors**. Mentors have more experience.

Apprentices watch their mentors. They copy them. They ask questions. They practice their skills.

They learn magic. They learn spells. They learn potions. They learn to control energy. They learn about nature. They learn about plants. They learn about the moon. Moon energy is powerful.

Witches have their own special spells and potions that they share with their apprentices.

Know the Lingo!

- **Alchemy:** turning one substance into another

- **Athame:** special blade with a black handle

- **Baculum:** wand

- **Bane:** bad, evil, destructive

- **Besom:** witch's broomstick

- **Boline:** curved blade

- **Compass round:** creating a boundary for magic to keep in the positive energy

- **Grimoire:** a notebook of magical spells

- **Incantation:** series of words said as a magic spell or charm

- **Necromancy:** talking to the dead to see into the future

- **Power hand:** the hand with which one normally writes and from which energy is sent

- **Seeker:** someone training to be a witch

- **Shaman:** healers and spiritual leaders in tribal societies

- **Sigil:** a symbol used for magic

- **Sorcery:** dangerous use of magic to cause harm

- **Stang:** a wooden pole with two or three prongs, used instead of a wand

- **Wortcunning:** herbal knowledge

Chapter
Five

Witch Hunts

What's the history of witches?
Why were witches hunted?

Witches were around in ancient times. Hecate was a Greek goddess. She was the goddess of witchcraft. She created the **jinx**. A jinx is bad luck.

Witchcraft was once real. It was "the Craft of the Wise." Witches were healers. They made natural medicine. They saved people's lives. They were leaders.

Then came organized religion. People followed religion. They didn't like witches. They wanted churchmen to heal. They thought witchcraft was evil. They thought witches worshipped the devil.

Before modern medicine, witches' healing powers seemed supernatural.

Real-World Connection

Wicca is pagan witchcraft. Pagan means not religious. Wiccans practice Wicca. They're known as "witches." Wiccans have their own beliefs. They have their own gods. Their symbol is a pentagram. This is a five-pointed star. They worship five elements: spirit, water, fire, earth, and air. They practice magic. They refer to the "Book of Shadows." It's a cookbook of spells. Wiccans have special ceremonies. They create a sacred circle. They cast "workings." These are spells. Their spells heal. They protect. They banish negative energy. They bring fertility. Fertility refers to babies and growth. They celebrate full moons. They also celebrate new moons. Some Wiccans work in the nude. This is known as skyclad. Some wear special robes. Some wear regular clothes. Witches live among us.

Two churchmen wrote a book. They did it in 1486. It promoted witch-hunting. It was based on a Bible line: "You shall not permit a **sorceress** to live." A sorceress is a female witch.

People hunted witches. They burned them. They stoned them. They drowned them. They did this in public. So witches hid.

Over 60,000 people were killed. They were accused of being witches. This happened from 1480 to 1750. This happened in Europe. This happened in North America.

Today, witches still inspire fear.

Fairy tales are filled with wicked witches.

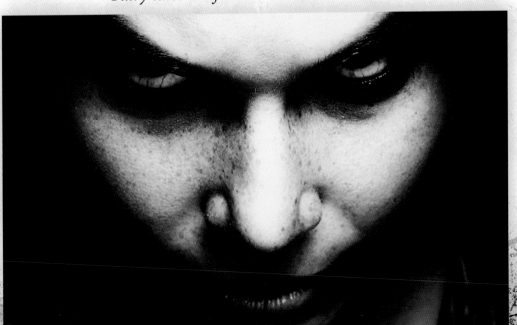

Did You Know?

- Thirteen is known as "the witching number." It's special. It's a good number. It's the number of full moons in a year.

- Sorcerers are the most powerful magicians. Wizards are second. Witches and warlocks are third.

- In Sweden, Easter is connected to witches. Swedish witches fly on broomsticks. They go to a mountain. They dance with the devil.

- Techno-witches use computers. They use technology instead of wands.

- Circe is a witch goddess. She turned men into animals. The first ballet was about her. The ballet was created in 1581.

- Many famous women were accused of being witches. An example is Catherine de Medici. Another example is Saint Joan of Arc.

- Many witches cast their spells at a fairy site. They believed this made their spells stronger.

- Witches celebrate more than just Halloween. They celebrate Beltane. It's the first day of May. They also celebrate Midsummer's Eve.

- Witchcraft is rooted in pagan beliefs. Pagans don't believe in Satan.

- Some believe you can see witches on Halloween. Wear your clothes backward. Or wear them inside out. Walk backward at the same time.

Consider This!

Take a Position: Some people think witches worship the devil. They ban anything to do with witches. They don't allow their children to read stories about witches. Do you think witch stories should be banned? Argue your point with reasons and evidence.

Say What? There are many witch characters from movies and television. Pick one. Compare that witch to the information presented in this book. Explain the similarities. Explain the differences. What accounts for the differences?

Think About It! There are mythical witches. There are "real" witches. They're known as Wiccans. This book focuses more on mythical witches. Why aren't there "real" wizards or warlocks?.

Learn More

- Bird, Malcolm. *The Witch's Handbook*. New York: Aladdin Books, 1988.

- Dickinson, Rachel. *The Witch's Handbook: A Field Guide to Magic*. New York: Price Stern Sloan, 2002.

- Samuels, L.T. *The Everything Kids' Witches and Wizards Book: Bewitch Your Friends, Bedazzle Your Parents, and Befuddle Your Enemies!* Avon, MA: Adams Media Corporation, 2000.

- Steer, Dugald. *Wizardology: The Book of the Secrets of Merlin*. Cambridge, MA: Candlewick Press, 2005.

Glossary

apprentices (uh-PREN-tis-iz) people who are training under more experienced people

blessings (BLES-ingz) good wishes

braids (BRAYDZ) things woven together

cast (KAST) to create

cauldrons (KAWL-druhnz) black cooking pots with three legs

charms (CHARMZ) magical objects that are tasked to do something

covens (KUH-vinz) groups of witches with 13 members

creed (KREED) rule or pledge

familiars (fuh-MIL-yurz) animals that serve witches

hags (HAGZ) old women

hereditary (huh-RED-ih-ter-ee) being born into something

hex (HEKS) to give a curse

jinx (JINKS) bad luck

mentors (MEN-terz) trainers, teachers

potions (POH-shunz) magical mixtures

power caps (POU-ur KAPS) limits to power

psychic (SYE-kik) related to the mind

runes (ROONZ) magical stones with symbols

scry (SKRI) to gaze into magical objects

sorceress (SOR-sur-uhs) a powerful female witch

spells (SPELZ) magical actions

spirits (SPIR-its) beings from another world

visions (VIZH-uhnz) signs or messages

wands (WAHNDZ) magical sticks

warlocks (WOR-loks) evil male witches

Index

About the Author

Dr. Virginia Loh-Hagan is an author, university professor, former classroom teacher, and curriculum designer. One of her favorite stories is *The Witches* by Roald Dahl. She lives in San Diego with her very tall husband and very naughty dogs. To learn more about her, visit www.virginialoh.com.